CONTENTS

College Budgeting And Lifestyle

Less Debt

Less Headache

More Fun

More Freedom

By

Mason Arthur

ABOUT THE BOOK

This book is for incoming college students, along with current undergraduate students. I'll be addressing some of the financial topics I wish I would've had a better understanding of before college began. The suggestions and information portrayed are part of my own experience through college and what I have found to work best along the way. I list several applications, tools, pieces of advice, and more that can be helpful in getting a head start on college budgeting, saving, and planning for the future. In no way, shape, or form am I given any compensation by these companies to promote their tools, unfortunately for me I suppose. Enjoy the read and hope you learn something new!

INTRODUCTION

College can be a tough journey for anyone, trying to figure out what you want to do for the rest of your life and land that dream job. It can be quite nerve-racking. You are heading into an unknown environment where the way of life is completely different from what you are accustomed to. It's also expensive. Thoughts may be creeping in the back of your mind on top of the rising cost of tuition and room and board. Will I gain the Freshman 15? (Freshman 15-referred to when first year college students gain weight. In this case, gain 15 pounds.) What if I'm not smart enough? Will I make any friends? What am I going to do now that I'm all on my own?

In this book, I am not saying you have to get 4-plus different jobs to stay afloat to have the least amount of debt possible. You don't need to avoid having fun, delightful times with friends to avoid being crushed by the never-ending student loan payments that are coming at you. On the contrary, I'm also not saying that you won't have to work at all to achieve a lifestyle that gives you the flexibility to enjoy college and get the most you can out of the experience. With a bit of preparation and following through with some fairly simple planning, college will be filled with less headaches and plenty of opportunities to build a tool set of skills that you can carry with you for the rest of your life.

Whether you're just starting to look at different choices of colleges to attend, about to step foot on campus for your first day, halfway through your undergrad journey, graduating soon, a concerned parent/guardian, or anyone interested in learning how to get through college while saving hundreds, maybe thousands, of dollars along the way will be able to take away valuable lessons. College is an investment in yourself, so as it goes with all investments, make this investment have the greatest returns.

Having financial talks with your parents, family members, and friends goes along with these ideas and tips to college budgeting that'll be presented to you. There's no one perfect way to stay on budget. By discussing this topic with others, it will make them aware of how prepared you are and hopefully they can provide insight to help you create some healthy money handling habits. Don't be afraid to reach out to those closest to you for help. The first time I talked to my family about budgeting as I prepared for college felt like I was speaking about something foreign or unknown. It felt weird to discuss a topic that I never really had to consider before. The good part about letting your family in on the decisions you're having to make creates an honest line of communication at no cost to you. When you have these conversations regularly, you will not feel petrified coming to talk to them again when you find yourself in a financial pickle.

Even though there may be no perfect way to keep track of expenses, you can ensure yourself that you'll be better prepared than the majority of students who do not follow a budget and, in turn, are stressed about finances. By focusing early and often on your financial future in college, you can start to build a steady reserve of cash and financial principles to begin your adult life.

FOCUSING ON A CAREER

If you think that you are going to keep the same major that you first enroll in and remain on a straight path to your dream job, you are likely to be strongly mistaken. Approximately 20-25% of students enter college as an 'Undecided' major. Around 75% of students change their major at least once in their studies (Freedman). This indecisiveness can come with a very high price tag. When you change majors in the middle of your undergraduate years, it means you will have to take more courses. This could potentially mean you have to stay in college another year, maybe more. Some scholarships and government grants only last four years, so the costs may increase exponentially after that. To avoid having to extend your time at college much longer than four years, a few pieces of advice may save you from doing a victory lap. (Victory Lap-refers to an undergraduate student having to go beyond the normal four years of studies to obtain a degree)

Self-evaluation, job shadowing, and research can reveal that you may be on a path to your dream job or on a path that does not lead to greener pastures.

Choosing a career path is a big commitment. You first and foremost want to find a major that is compatible with your goals and talents. Gather information about yourself. What do you like to do in your spare time? What are you good at? Focus on values that are important to you, along with things that keep your interest, such as that driving or motivational force behind what you're passionate for. There are plenty of self-assessment tools out there to help you evaluate yourself. The Myers-Briggs Type Indicator is one of the most popular free personality assessments out there. It provides you information behind whether you lean towards being an introvert or extrovert, sensing or intuition, thinking or feeling, and judgment or perception. These characteristics are explained in more detail once you take the test. No one tool will have all of the answers, but if you try several, and they keep telling you the same information, it could be a signal as to what you might want to pursue.

Job shadowing is a great indicator into whether you'll like a certain job or not. Spending a day in the life of someone who has been working in the career you want will open your eyes into if this is really something worth pursuing yourself. Job shadowing is very helpful for those in the 'Undecided' major category. You could watch a nurse make their rounds to different patients on their floor, study building types with an architectural engineer, or follow the life in the day of a business manager. To start job shadowing, reach out to a person that has the job you want, or reach out to the company that has the job to ask about shadowing someone for the day. Companies are generally accommodating towards your request.

Research the types of jobs you can get with the major you want to pursue. My major, for instance, was Management Information Systems (MIS). I could lean towards being a software developer, which builds applications by coding. I could be an analyst, which communicates how different technology systems are interacting with one another. I could also go into a different job within the realm of business since an MIS degree is in the College of Business. Technology has always intrigued me, so I knew this route would be something that fit my personality, even if I couldn't make up my mind which specific major I wanted to be right away.

At any school and especially bigger schools, they will have several majors that require relatively the same classes, so switching majors halfway through would only require a few additional classes to graduate on time. As in my example above, let's say you want to go into the corporate world and major in Business but don't know what to specialize in (accounting, finance, marketing, information systems, etc.). The first year or two will require you to take the same classes as any Business major. At that point, you can take feedback from fellow classmates and peers, do more research, and truly see if what you were originally wanting to specialize in is still the career for you. If you're major is too specialized and the school you're attending does not offer alternatives if you decided to switch from that major, you better make sure that your major leads you to the job you desire. Following your own self-evaluation, job shadowing, and research process can help boost your confidence with such a big decision.

CHOOSING A COLLEGE

You should be thinking about what kind of tuition, room, and board you're going to have to pay off before you even step foot on a college campus. There are several strategies to reduce the risk of spending way more than you can afford to get that degree. The average debt a college graduate has is $33,310. Out of the 42.9 million student loan borrowers, 2.7 million owe $100,000+ (Carter). Strive to be under that average debt benchmark. I would even challenge you to strive for a plan that has zero student loan debt come graduation. In many scenarios, this is not realistic. However, It is very possible to keep your student loans to a level that will take 5 years or less to pay off. Odds are you don't want to be paying your loans off a decade or two after you received that precious piece of paper called a diploma. Unfortunately, that is the case for many. Choosing a college and major that fits your budget, career, lifelong goals is a serious step in shaping what kind of financial situation you'll be in 10, 20, or even 30 years down the road.

Many high school kids often focus most of their attention on the top schools they can get into, and while it is a good idea to reach out and beyond for the best education you can get, sometimes that hefty price tag will get thrown under the rug when it shouldn't be. I'll talk more about financial aid offered to you in the next chapter, but to start off, be aware of the total costs that tuition will burden you with. A frightening fact shows that 59%, a strong majority, of millennials graduating have no clue when their student loans will be paid off (CollegeQuest).

When choosing a college, take into account the total net cost of tuition, room, and board. This would be the total gross amount of attending school, subtracting out any scholarships or grants you may receive. This leaves you in the ballpark of the amount of money that will still be owed during the tenure of college.

Shop around. You spend time looking for the best option on a new car, go to the mall to find the greatest deal on a pair of jeans, or analyze the product reviews that people post before your next spur of the moment purchase on Amazon. I had an initial list of six colleges I wanted to attend, mainly based off of location and major requirements they met. From there, I narrowed it down to two schools I would seriously consider. These schools were the ones I would take the time to do a campus visit with, talk to some of the professors of the major(s) I was interested in, ask about financial aid packages, and more. Any more than two or three serious contenders would have made my decision immensely more difficult.

Out of the two schools that I was seriously considering, one was an Out-Of-State university and the other was an In-State school. Out-Of-State and In-State tuition vary significantly. Out-Of-State tuition is usually higher because you are not a resident of the state in which you'd be attending. The main reason In-State public schools give you a lower cost burden is an incentive since you have been indirectly funding the public schools and universities through State taxes every year. If you are not positive on what kind of major you'd like to pursue, an In-State college may be your better bet. It would give you a less stressful option to potentially change your major. As in, your wallet may forgive you more if you have to go an extra semester or two at an In-State school since it's generally a lower tuition cost. Don't be afraid of considering an Out-Of-State school however. Out-Of-State schools offer an abundance of scholarships aimed towards Out-Of-State students, which can sometimes make up for the higher tuition cost.

Out-Of-State versus In-State tuition only applies to public universities. Private universities have students pay more regardless since they are unable to receive any of the tax moneys from the government. Private schools tend to have a smaller head count and less career paths to choose from while public schools can have a wider range of classes and people. A good look at your total budget, the kind of culture or environment you want to be a part of, and size of class are all excellent factors in determining the type of experience you want out of college.

Some universities urge students to apply and make an "early decision" to attend. This happens around the November-December time frame the year before you attend college. This means you are no longer able to apply to any other schools. While this may be perceived as giving you a better chance at being admitted, that may not always be the case. Early decision admission rates vary from school to school. There may be no penalty for backing out of an early decision if you have a valid reason, such as, the financial package is not as great as you were hoping, or a family member is deeply ill and you're unable to attend as a result. However, it does not look good on your high school, yourself, and you may not get a deposit back, if required, for rescinding an early decision. If you're set on a school and get accepted at the beginning of your senior year of high school with a lot of confidence in your decision, making an early decision may be the right option for you. For many students, it would be wise to weigh the costs and benefits of attending multiple colleges. The financial aid packages can make or break your top picks.

SCHOLARSHIPS AND FINANCIAL AID

My best advice for scholarships is to apply for all of them. Fill out an application for every single one you possibly can and then some. It's essentially free money to help pay for your education. Is there an $100 scholarship at your school that you think, "Is this really worth my time and energy to apply for?" Generally, scholarship applications only take an hour or two to complete if you devote the time and energy to them. Would you turn down $100/hour of your time? Probably not unless you're a Vanderbilt.

Open yourself up to different kinds of scholarships. Merit scholarships are the most common, being offered to those that surpass the standards given out in the scholarship details. This would include academic achievements and would also include those needing financial assistance. Other types of scholarships aim at particular groups. As a kid that grew up participating in agricultural classes, I qualified for the Future Farmers of America (FFA) scholarship. Women, minorities, military personnel and family, and all sorts of different backgrounds can gain access to these specific group scholarships.

There are certain types of scholarships that can be applied for each semester or year. These renewable scholarships, while they may sound environmentally friendly, are actually great scholarships to be applying for. Be sure to watch out for those application dates and set a reminder on your phone to reapply when the time comes. I had a scholarship where I would have to turn my transcript in each semester, and as long as the grades met the required level, I would keep getting scholarship dollars. For scholarships that involve writing an essay, keep past scholarship essays saved in a file or folder because you may be able to use the same essay, or tweak it just a bit to apply again for a different scholarship.

A few things you need to keep in mind as you get ready to fill out scholarship applications: letters of recommendation, scholarship award amounts, and too good to be true scenarios. A good letter of recommendation will go a long way in the eyes of a scholarship giver. Whether it be a classroom teacher, coach, or mentor, give the person, who is taking time out of their day to write about you, plenty of time to complete their part.

The high dollar scholarships can be quite tempting, but the Mega Millions lottery is also tempting, and you won't see me investing my time into that instead of my day job. To reduce the size of the competition and increase your odds, smaller scholarships award a better chance for you to win. By winning several smaller scholarships, the money could surpass applying for one big scholarship that has less likelihood of paying off. However, if you have the time, then definitely apply for those larger scholarships. The best strategy after all is to apply for them all and cover the cost of school as much as possible.

Financial aid gives you the support needed to get by in college without having to drop out. Expenses can start piling up faster than you are able to pay them off. Federal financial aid can be received from filling out the Free Application for Federal Student Aid (FAFSA), which is a free form that needs to be filled out each year (Best Schools). The federal government provides a majority of the financial aid in the U.S. Similar to the federal level, there's State and college/institution aid that come in the form of grants, scholarships, or work-study programs, which help students who want to work part-time with education costs. Private aid can come from local businesses, churches, service organizations, etc. in the form of either loans or scholarships. Talk with your high school guidance counselor, university financial aid office, or gather information online to see what aid is out there. When it comes to college, I've found you have to take the initiative to do the research or start the conversation with these folks. Once they see you're interested, they will provide you with multiple resources and also be more willing to go out of their way help you than if you say nothing and wonder why you had little to no chances for different financial aid offerings.

Be cautious as you review financial aid offerings. Federal loans can trick you into thinking these loans are grants or free financial aid. Financial aid, like a Federal Stafford Loan and Pell Grant, could be offered to you. While a Federal Stafford Loan is a government lower interest rate loan, some people may mistake the loan for financial aid that does not need paid back. It is still a loan. The money needs to be paid back to the government with interest. A Pell Grant on the other hand is essentially free government money that helps reduce your tuition, and the best part is that it does not have to be paid back.

Pay close attention when accepting any financial aid and know the terms of the type of aid you are accepting. In the end, I would have gone through my college years with a seemingly never-ending trail of debt if I had not applied for as much financial aid as I could.

PREPARING A PLAN

It all starts with a mindset. This mindset consists of remembering why you're going to college in the first place. College gives us the opportunities and challenges to grow into the adults we want to be. Adulting is coming quicker than you think, and when that mid-life point in your life hits, it's almost too late to recover if only poor, inadequate preparation in handling the challenges life throws at you is taken.

Grow those key skills to become the best you can be to prepare for that dream job. College education serves us well in this aspect, but why turn down the chance to grow other skills that are just beginning to develop at the same time? Budgeting and financial skills... For me, college was the first time I ever even had to think about a budget. Many students, and surprisingly many adults, do not have a plan for managing where their money is coming and going. You do not have to be a rocket scientist or major in mathematics to develop a solid budget that gives you the control you need to handle your finances.

"Keep It Simple Stupid." A quote from one of my favorite comedy shows, The Office, serves its purpose here. Keep the pieces of a budget simple enough for you to pick up and maintain. Break the budget down, starting with a semester. While adults generally budget annually, I found it much easier to break it down by semester in college. You can break it down as you please. A good place to start with budgeting is to list down all of your revenue and expenses. As a college student, it is likely that you will be having quite a few expenses during this period of time. Tracking these expenses helps to not only stay organized but may give you a bit of a wakeup call as to how much money you're laying down on the table invest in your education. Tuition, room, and board can stack on quickly, and four years of expenses can stack up to tens of thousands of dollars in debt. While there are many bad kinds of debt, like credit card debt with high interest rates, student loan debt is not a thrilling debt to be paying off monthly for 10, 20, or even 30 years. You will have house payments, car payments, and possibly even children to support down the road.

With all of the technology and applications out there today, I still believe listing all income, expenses, and savings yourself is the simplest way to get all categories out there in front of your eyes. It can also be the easiest and most accessible way to keep track of all budgeting categories over an extended period of time: tuition, food, room, school supplies, textbooks, personal essentials, extracurricular fees, and transportation to name a few. Microsoft has a simple, accessible Excel application that is compatible with your phone and tablet. I use the computer, but a phone or tablet would work just as easily for all of the basic purposes outlined here.

Sample Excel: Expenses and Income

	A	B	C	D	E	F
1	Income		Expenses		Savings	
2	Scholarships		Tuition		Emergency	
3	Work		Housing		Spring Break	
4	Allowance		Utilities		Post Grad	
5			Textbooks			
6			Food			
7			Car			
8			Personal			
9			Entertainment			
10			Miscellaneous			
11						

Saving money may sound like an impossible task when you already have an abundance of expenses waiting to be paid off. Luckily, there are some applications out there that have an easy, hands-off way of allowing the savings to build up slowly but surely. Acorn is a free application for college students that have a *.edu* mail address, and the free subscription lasts four years from the sign-up date. After those four years are up, it costs $1-3 a month depending on the type of account you have. Its main principle is to save the change you make on everyday expenses. For instance, let's say you're filling up with gas and it costs $25.75. Acorn rounds this up to $26.00, and the difference of $0.25 goes into savings. In the app, you have the ability to choose from different investment portfolios (Investment Portfolio- A collection of assets. The most common assets being securities, which stocks, mutual funds, and bonds.). You can choose a more conservative or more aggressive approach, whichever suits your comfort level. I used this for a few years while it was free, then moved my savings from this account elsewhere to avoid having to pay the management fee each month. I enjoyed using this service during college, where I would make many smaller purchases and the savings would continue to build up without me having to monitor it at all. I would save around $10 a month with auto investing on Acorn. This is a great way to save on top of whatever you may be putting in your checking or savings account.

Mint is a very useful budgeting application if you decide you'd rather have a strictly budget focused app to assist in money managing compared to Excel. I surely won't be offended. College is all about learning what works for you, especially with financial management. Mint is a product of Intuit, a group that has also made TurboTax, ProConnect, and Quickbooks a success. You are able to link up your banks and credit card accounts securely to a Mint account. The app categorizes each expense you make on your credit card; you can track where your money is going each month. While good financial tools are out there, there are an equally number of bad ones looking to make some money off of your hard earned money. Do your research before picking a random one up and deciding you dislike all budget applications because one spoiled the pot. I will be sticking with Excel for many of my references in using a budget. It's free, convenient, and easy to modify to fit your needs.

The plan finally comes into play by beginning to estimate where your money will go before it happens, hence the term, budget. This should be a simple guesstimate of tracking your expenses. Create a plan that has the flexibility to adjust to changing circumstances. College tends to throw you many curveballs, so sometimes having a strict plan that never adjusts is just not feasible. Your car breaks down and you're late for class. A friend wants to catch up, so you go out for some drinks and an Italian cuisine. You need a new laptop due to that darn coffee cup not being on tight enough. Things like these can and are bound to happen out of the blue. Life happens.

A plan helps ease the stress when life does happen. Try adding a budget plan to the list you made of income, expenses, and savings. This plan needs to be as detailed as you want it to be and needs to capture where all of your money is going to achieve the most success of following through with it. The more educated you become at setting your budget, the less headaches you will receive when the unexpected life situations become reality because you are prepared.

Sample Budget Plan: A guesstimate of expenses

	A	B	C	D	E	F
1	Income	Monthly Guesstimate	Expenses	Monthly Guesstimate	Savings	Monthly Guesstimate
2	*Scholarships	$1,000.00	*Tuition	$2,500.00	Emergency	$50.00
3	Work	$320.00	*Housing	$750.00	Spring Break	$30.00
4	*Allowance	$500.00	Utilities	$100.00	Post Grad	$40.00
5			*Textbooks	$125.00		
6			Food	$200.00		
7			Car	$150.00		
8			Personal	$100.00		
9			Entertainment	$100.00		
10			Miscellaneous	$50.00		
11						
12						
13	*Note Values: (Semesters are based over a 4 month timeline)					
14	Semester Scholarships - $4,000					
15	Semester Allowance - $2,000					
16	Semester Tuition - $10,000					
17	Semester Housing - $3,000					
18	Semester Textbooks - $500					

You can be as creative as needed to get your budget plan to a place where you like it. I decide not to include loans on this plan because any student loans are not really income as they need to be paid back in the end. You can include them if you'd prefer. Loans would fit as an additional income to match whatever expenses that cannot be covered by scholarships, work, or allowance. I will go into the specifics on each category of income, expenses, and savings to give a better understanding of what each line item in the plan encompasses.

The scholarships line item lumps in any scholarships along with grants or financial aid. These should not have to be paid back to anyone. The work item comprises of any on campus job or additional income you work towards while attending school. Allowance includes any money your parents/guardians give you towards your education. This could be in the form of paying for the monthly rent at your apartment or giving you a certain amount of money for food.

Tuition is the cost to attend classes and is provided by the university prior to each semester. Housing can be referred to as room and board, if you are living on campus. This would mean housing and utilities would be lumped together since students living on campus do not have to pay utilities. Utilities apply to off campus students the most, which include the costs of gas, electric, water, cable, and internet on top of whatever the cost of housing/rent is. Textbooks can include physical or online books, any instructional material a professor requests, and any classroom materials needed like folders and journals. Textbooks can also include any technology needed to participate in classes. Nowadays, a computer or some form of technology to connect to the Internet is needed to do homework or take tests. Food purchases can be either grocery store items or going out to eat. Filling up with gas, changing the oil, and getting the car serviced would go towards car or transportation expenses. Personal items can be taken different ways: shopping for clothes, personal care like shampoo, or buying a random item for yourself on eBay. Movies, nights out with some buds, bowling, golfing, and plenty more activities like that are considered entertainment. A miscellaneous item can cover anything that doesn't quite fit into any of the categories listed above.

The ability to save really builds tremendous willpower and talent leading into adult life. Saving up for things like spring break, an emergency, and post-graduation gives a sense of comfort that you will be financially covered when the time comes. As the book progresses, I will dive into each of the bigger items on the list to give tips and suggestions on how to handle the categories of income, expenses, and savings.

Here are a few tips as you're jotting the plan down that will keep you motivated and willing to commit to this plan: create target dates, treat yourself, and add an accountable friend.

I go with monthly target dates, but you can schedule it out how you like. The same time each month keeps it consistent as a simple way to review your budget. This allows you enough time to not have to constantly look at your budget, and at the same time, it makes you review your expenses several times during the semester. You may have to adjust where you allocate your money. The first time you guesstimate you may say you only need $100 for food a month, when in reality, it may be more like $150-$200 a month as the groceries and dining out start to add up. You may not travel home or drive off of campus as much as you initially thought, so that $200 a month for gas may come down to $100 a month.

If you stay within your budget, or fairly close to it (I like giving myself a 10% over budget leeway in case something out of the ordinary happens), treat yourself to a night out on the town for committing to your plan. Don't go breaking the bank at the fanciest steakhouse restaurant, but a movie theater with some buttery popcorn or going out with some buds can be a fun way to celebrate being fiscally responsible.

Having a friend, roommate, classmate, or anyone to join you on this journey can help them out and keep you both more accountable to stay on track. A partner in this endeavor is certainly not a necessity but may prove helpful in motivating yourself to stick to the budget. I was fortunate to have a financially responsible roommate in college, who'd join me in creating his own budget. He'd be the reasonable one and keep me in check when I'd get those impulse spending moments. For example, when I was looking to buy a new set of golf clubs, he'd say, "Don't you already have a decent bag of clubs right now?" Having a budget partner, whether they're financially savvy or not, will still be a good way for you to talk to another person about your spending habits and where you can both improve. Any good partnership will help pick the other person up when their struggling and help celebrate the successes together when all is well.

FOLLOWING THROUGH WITH THE PLAN

A plan is only as good as its execution. You have the college set in stone. You have the budget and expenses set, which may include some financial aid to get you through the next four years. Now this is the hardest part, maintaining and keeping up with your plan. It's like the New Year's resolution to get ready for summer by working on your beach body. It's a nice thing to say you're going to do, but it's an entirely different thing to actually do it. The great part about maintaining a budget is that it doesn't take as long as a workout and sweating is generally not involved, unless you really broke the budget. In that case, you may need to make a new plan anyways.

I would take a brief moment out of the month, anywhere from 10-20 minutes on the first Sunday of the month, to keep up with my finances. This would make reviewing the previous month of expenses easier in order to see if I'm on track to hit the budget for the current month and semester. If you're in a Netflix state of mind, you'll spend less than half an episode a month of your favorite TV drama series dedicating yourself to staying on track and being financially responsible.

Sample Budget Plan: A view of expenses and income that have occurred

	Income	Monthly Guesstimate	Monthly Actuals	% on Budget	Expenses	Monthly Guesstimate	Monthly Actuals	% on Budget	Savings	Monthly Guesstimate	Monthly Actuals
1		A	B	C	D	E	F	G	H	I	J	K
1	Income	Monthly Guesstimate	Monthly Actuals	% on Budget	Expenses	Monthly Guesstimate	Monthly Actuals	% on Budget	Savings	Monthly Guesstimate	Monthly Actuals
2	*Scholarships	$1,000.00	$1,000.00	100	*Tuition	$2,500.00	$2,500.00	100	Emergency	$50.00	$50.00
3	Work	$320.00	$350.00	109	*Housing	$750.00	$750.00	100	Spring Break	$30.00	$50.00
4	*Allowance	$500.00	$500.00	100	Utilities	$100.00	$105.45	105	Post Grad	$40.00	$50.00
5					*Textbooks	$125.00	$125.00	100			
6					Food	$200.00	$189.56	95			
7					Car	$150.00	$125.27	84			
8					Personal	$100.00	$98.80	99			
9					Entertainment	$100.00	$51.93	52			
10					Miscellaneous	$50.00	$25.00	50			
11											
12	Note: The calculations for comparing Actuals against Guesstimates are only estimates. Feel free to use this method as a guide as you prepare to execute your budget plan.
13											

TARGET MONEY FLOW	ACTUAL MONEY FLOW	OUT OF or WITHIN BUDGET
-$2,255.00	-$2,121.01	-$133.99

Note: The goal is to have an Actual Money Flow greater than or equal to the Target Money Flow to stay within budget.

The spreadsheet looks at the budget plan or guesstimates against the actual values for the month. This is essentially the minimum needed to see what you planned to spend at the beginning of the month versus how you are actually spending your money. As you can see, you will likely have a negative number as student loans are not included in this calculation. If you're bringing in more income than the total amount of expenses without taking out any loans, you may be on track to a debt free college experience. The goal is to have the actual money flow be relatively similar, ideally within 10%, of your target money flow. It is always better to have the actual money flow be greater than the target money flow. In this example, the -$2,121.01 actual money flow is greater than the -$2,255.00 target money flow in the example above. In other words, this means you were within the budget by $133.99 compared to what you targeted to spend. You spent $133.99 less than what you gave yourself to spend for the month.

This kind of execution requires a bit of leg work to start off. Once you have a method down for recording your actual income and expenses, keeping track takes little to no time at all. Look at how much you brought in working this month. See what kind of charges you put on your credit card for food and entertainment costs. You can get as in-depth and creative as you want with keeping track of the budget.

I also like to have a weekly plan of objectives as a reminder to stay focused and on the right track, basically a weekly list of budgetary goals to strive for. This thought process may help you as you build out your monthly guesstimate budget as well. Set some attainable benchmarks for the week. A week ahead you can generally predict what kind of life events will occur over the following week. Give yourself a buffer. You don't want to set unrealistic expectations or else the motivation to stick to a budget will slowly fade away. For me, the odds that I would only go out to eat once a week were pretty slim, considering my subpar cooking skills. If I set that type of goal for myself, I would likely fail week after week. To set myself up for a challenge while staying within expectations, I would limit myself to dining out for 2-3 meals per week. This is perfectly reasonable and forces me to cook a couple meals during the week rather than eating out every day. I suggest writing these objectives down in a planner, journal, or note on your phone. Write it down somewhere that is accessible and somewhere you see this list frequently as a reminder. Research has found that writing things down helps you remember better, so help yourself out. That's also a good note for when you struggle to pay attention in class. Those two-hour lectures can get a bit dry. The more you write down, the more you are likely to digest and retain.

Sample Weekly Objectives List

Weekly Budget Objectives

~Entertainment costs should be $25 or less.
~Limit dining out to 2-3 times per week.
~Put away $30 from work into savings.
~Any spare change goes into a jar for savings.
~Give $10 to charity or church.

Picture yourself completing the objective. It feels good to meet those goals. You don't want to make your goals too big or too unrealistic to the point that it stresses you out. If the goals are too small or non-existent, no motivation will be there to stick to the budget. The willpower to stay away from going on a shopping spree is easier when you visualize your long-term goals of becoming a financially independent adult that doesn't live by paying off one credit card debt to the next. To reiterate, having a companion, or a few people you can talk to about your financial plan and the progress of it, is a good way to build up accountability in yourself. For me, it was a few people. My coworkers and roommates on campus, who worked, studied, and experienced relatively the same things I was going through, and my parents, who gave financial advice from afar. You don't want to come back to those people at the end of the month or semester and say you didn't care about your budget or spent double what you were planning to spend. You'd like to tell them how you had that will-power and motivation to stick to a plan and keep on track.

HOUSING

Room and board can vary by college, but the price between living in the dorms and living off of campus is widespread. I found it to be around a thousand dollars more expensive to live on campus than off campus per semester. With that being said, I do highly recommend living on campus for your first year, even two years, of college. Students who stay on campus for the first two years have a much higher percentage of finishing out their degree than students who live off campus right from the start. Being able to participate in student activities, meet new friends/roommates, and utilize campus amenities like transportation is much easier while living on campus.

On campus housing has a set budget because everything is paid upfront. Room and utility costs are a fixed expense set by the university before a student even steps foot in their room. Your education can benefit from being on campus. Everyone in the dorms is experiencing college and the burden of class work and exams together, which tends to create a better studying mentality. You will likely have a shorter walk or commute to classes. Meal plans are offered as a packaged deal for living on campus. On campus housing is great for incoming students, as many of the adulting tasks are likely still handled by the university. They make your meals, clean, take out the trash, and provide transportation.

Living off campus is another story. It does not have the convenience of being right next to your classroom buildings. Many times, it's harder to participate in on campus student activities and to meet new friends every year like the dorms would provide. You will either have to buy a meal plan or buy and make your own food. While these may seem like downfalls to living off campus, there are several benefits to living off campus.

Off campus housing is generally cheaper as many of the costs are actual instead of fixed like it is on campus. For example, your meal plan may be a fixed amount, and you have to use the whole plan up or you're essentially losing out on money. Whereas when you buy groceries on your own, you control exactly what you buy, an actual amount, and will consume what you purchase. Living off campus teaches you a great deal about many of the responsibilities that adults have to deal with, which makes you a more independent individual. You'll likely experience paying monthly utilities for the first time (gas, electric, water, and Internet). You'll learn what happens if the electric bill doesn't get paid. Lights out. You will have more freedom to do what you want when you want in the privacy of your own place. No more pesky room rules or tons of people to distract you like a dorm might have. You won't have to move out of your place after the academic year. If you need to take summer classes or have a summer job in the same city where you attend college, having an off campus rental allows you to come and go during the year as long as you're paying rent. And finally, you can comfortably choose who you want to live with rather than being assigned with someone randomly, as is the case most of the times in dorms. There are plenty of benefits to both on and off campus housing. I strongly encourage you to try both sides of housing throughout your college experience.

Having roommates is an easy way to cut the costs of living down. It can cost hundreds of dollars more per month to live on your own. Share the cost burden of renting a place with friends. They can help decrease the costs of monthly rent and utilities.

Housing can make or break your bank depending on where you want to live. The higher monthly price tag for safe and comfortable housing might be worthwhile if your college is in a big city or in an area where crime is not uncommon. This shouldn't serve as an alarming factor to pay thousands of dollars more to live in the nicest, most secure apartment complexes but as something to think about. In general, if you live on campus or in off campus housing within a few blocks of your campus, you should be able to find a housing situation that fits into your budget and meets your safety and comfort level. Campus police make an environment that is safer for students. I found affordable housing that was right next to the nice fancy apartment complexes for nearly half the cost. That's the difference of paying $500 a month versus paying $1000 a month. The money saved on housing could go towards splurging a bit on food and groceries.

FOOD

My favorite topic to discuss comes with some harsh realities. I hate to say it, but you may want to break some of your regular, and possibly unnecessary, food/drink spending habits. If you can't live without it, try limiting yourself. A few days of the week that you stroll out of bed, hop in the car, and get your Starbucks coffee, try making your own coffee or go without it. The days that you have the willpower to go without? Put the money that you would have spent on a coffee into a jar or savings, where you can visually see how much money you're saving by not succumbing to a spending habit. To make a cup of coffee at home costs around $0.50 compared to at least a $2.00+ purchase at Starbucks, saving you over $500 annually if that's a daily routine.

Try to limit the amount of times per week you eat out. The costs can surprisingly add up quickly. Not only is cooking at home cheaper, it's generally healthier because you control the ingredients going into the foods you prepare, whereas restaurants can add plenty of sugars, extra calories, and sodium to your diet. Our Millennial generation is way more likely to dine out than the generations before.

Take making some chicken parmigiana for an example. Olive Garden, don't get me wrong I love everything about the place and don't even get me started on the breadsticks, has a chicken parmigiana entree for $16, which means $20+ when you include the tip. This can serve as probably two meals because when you eat at Olive Garden you generally fill up on the soup, salad, and breadsticks as you wait for the entree to be served. Two servings for $10 a serving is what that Olive Garden experience comes out to. By making your own, it can be way cheaper. Four chicken breasts, an egg, butter, spaghetti sauce, mozzarella and Parmesan cheese, olive oil, and pasta all bought at Aldi's costs around $10. This is four servings of food for $2.50 a piece, a quarter of the amount it would be at Olive Garden. You even have leftover ingredients to make another Italian masterpiece.

Another benefit of making food at home is that it is much easier to keep the leftovers for another meal. At a restaurant, I sometimes feel obligated to eat the entire plate of food, otherwise it'll go to waste. You put all that hard work into making a meal. Why not put in a little more effort to make a bigger portion and save the extras? There are obvious cost benefits to having leftovers as a great way to make two or three meals out of one. I'm not saying that you shouldn't go out to eat at all because I definitely understand the cravings one might have for some Chick-Fil-A nuggets and sauce, but it'd definitely help your wallet to learn to cook a few meals by yourself to get by. By eating out once or twice a week, I treat dining out as a reward rather than a habit.

If you live on campus and/or have a meal plan, take advantage of it the best you can. If you're fortunate to go to a school with multiple on campus dining options or the option to use your meal plan at other restaurants, eat at those places as much as you can for the sake of your budget. You may need to break out of the routine and get some Piada or Steak-N-Shake occasionally, but upfront you already paid for this meal plan. Not using the plan to its fullest is like throwing money down the drain. It's like buying 20 pizzas from Pizza Hut for the semester, and you get one of the pizzas from Pizza Hut at any time you want. However, if you don't pick up your 20 pizzas throughout the semester, you cannot go back and redeem any of the money from the pizzas you did not order. It's gone. To use the meal plan up by the end of the semester, I would purchase snacks from the on campus convenience store that allowed me to use my meal plan dining dollars to load my fridge, so instead of having to buy from a vending machine or another store with my own money, I would use the meal plan in which I've already paid.

When you decide to eat out, here are a couple tips that may lighten up the costs. The app, Hooked, is a great college food and bar deal finder, usually found in bigger campus settings. The deals change constantly. It makes you try different restaurants with your friends. All you have to do is show the cashier or waiter before you pay, and you'll get to redeem the deal. For those who go to the same restaurant frequently, another piece of advice I like is to download that restaurant's app and make an account. Many food places have rewards programs. It takes a minute or two to make an account ordinarily, and if you order from the same restaurant 5-10 times you start to get either free food or a great discounted deal.

TEXTBOOKS

If you think the cost of tuition is rising at a fast rate, textbooks are getting pricier even quicker. The key to passing many classes requires the purchase of one or two of these. Nowadays, most books are sold in an online format instead of the physical hardback option. Textbook providers get you to come back to them each and every semester by using online codes to register yourself for a session. These unique codes mean you have to pay for the book and code together. Very seldom are the days where you can use someone else's book from a previous semester in that same class for the next semester.

If there is not a unique code and the book edition of the textbook doesn't matter or hasn't changed, you could look into purchasing the book from a classmate who's taken the class before. This way is preferred as it's probably the cheapest route, depending on how close you are to the person you're getting the book from.

The easiest and most convenient way to purchase a textbook is at the campus bookstore. This also happens to be the most expensive option. Sometimes it is absolutely necessary to buy books from the campus bookstore. Whether it be a class lab workbook or other specific items requested by the professor, you may need to go to the bookstore to buy specialized material. A majority of the time, you can avoid having to purchase from a bookstore if it's a book that is widely known or that many universities use. Buy a used book instead by searching for its ISBN number. This will get you the correct author and edition. Save yourself quite a bit of money, and you can get used books in good condition.

Sometimes splitting a book with a close friend or classmate taking the same class is also an option. As a side note, you may want to see if your professor needs you to have your book in front of you during class, in which you may want to have your own. You may also like marking up a book because highlighting helps you study better, so sharing may not be the best option. Sharing does split the costs and helps you keep in touch with someone else in the class to keep each other accountable for tests and homework.

Renting a book is another option that may make financial sense. If the cost of a new or used book is a few hundred dollars, renting a book for less than half the cost of buying the book would likely save you money. I preferred this option when I had a choice. You would get a book in nice condition, and when you're done with the semester, simply turn it back into where you purchase it from. You don't have to mess with trying to resell the book after the semester is over. Chegg is a very user-friendly book rental company and many times cheaper than Amazon. Returning a rental after use is free, and you have the option to purchase the book when you're done with the class instead.

A good rule of thumb is to wait until your first day of class to hear from the professor him or herself to see if the textbook is necessary. The syllabus may outline the book being used for the class, but the professor may say otherwise if the book is absolutely necessary. Unless the syllabus says the textbook is necessary or the professor emails before classes begin to say you need to purchase the book or an online code, it is best to wait and see if the book is required to do well in the class.

JOBS AND CASH INFLOWS

For most of this book, we have discussed ways you can save money, but how about, how can you make money? There are several different routes you can take as a college student. Finding a job that suits you and your comfort level of managing a part-time job and part-time student lifestyle is up to you.

On campus jobs offer several different opportunities for you to be able to gain a bit of side income while you complete your studies. Many colleges have job boards where you can see many of the listings for positions available on campus. Look for something that you may have had a knack for in high school, like working at a cafe because you really love coffee, or for something you wouldn't mind doing as a break from your studies, like being a lifeguard by working on the university's fitness staff. For me, I was fortunate to get a job in my university's athletic department, which fulfilled my passion for sports. If one of your classmates or roommates has a nice gig, ask them what they had to do to get that job. They might be a good reference when you apply and make it easier for you to get that same job. If you excel in one of your classes and get along with your professor, you could ask the professor to be a Teaching Assistant (TA). Students can become TA's to grade papers, help teach the class in smaller class sizes, and provide any assistance the professor may need in teaching the class. After your first year on campus, you could apply to become a Resident Assistant (RA). RA's can get their room paid for in exchange for the time and effort devoted to helping out other students in their dorm halls, keeping them safe, and being there as someone that these students can talk to.

If you're anything like me, you may have not had a formal interview process before college. My resume was not up to par with other students' resumes. Your Career Services office is a great service to help you with exactly that, landing a job. Part of their help can consist in helping you form a resume, either for a job during undergrad or after you graduate.

You'll want to think of a job during your undergraduate experience as something that will help you begin your career after graduation and stand out in the job you wish to have in the future. I was hesitant working in the Athletic Department, which included working with sports camps the university held for kids K-12. It seemed to have nothing to do with my passion for Information Technology. However, as I progressed through my undergraduate experience, working more and more with sports camps, it was easy for me to succeed in providing customer service not only to the children at the camps but their parents as well. From being a rather shy kid in high school, I was able to build up the confidence to pursue a career where my job is all about communication while working in Information Technology. The moral is to think about your on campus job as something much more meaningful than an ordinary on campus job.

You do not necessarily have to land a job on campus either. It's more convenient in larger cities to find a plethora of jobs available around town. Smaller schools will have these opportunities as well but may be harder to come by. Using the knowledge you already have, since you made it to this point and you're in college, you could serve as a tutor to other college students or to kids K-12 in the surrounding areas. You can generally make up your own schedule, and the students learning from you have to show up on your time. This is nice for someone looking to teach something they have a passion for. Some girls would take the opportunity to nanny children when they were not in classes. Working adults need nannying services any time, day or night. If you're free on the weekend and wouldn't mind watching a kid or two, you could make some easy cash and maybe even be lucky enough to have some spare time while the kids are napping or sleeping. If you're finding it hard to get a job in the evening or on weekends, restaurant waiters and waitresses are in high demand. This type of job grants you the patience and energy to deal with customers firsthand. Impress your customers with charm and politeness, and you could receive a generous tip in return. Plus, you'll eventually have to impress a boss or coworkers in your career, so you might as well get some practice in the meantime.

Some students can choose not to have a job while in college. This is perfectly reasonable. Some majors require nothing but devotion and your time in order to get passing grades, and a job is not feasible. Having a job during your college years helps generate a bit of side income, but it also allows you to experience something in college that many kids may not have experienced. You have to be motivated to handle transitioning between studying and working. This can become a bit stressful. Time management is an important aspect of your lifestyle if you choose to juggle a job and school. You may have to plan a week or two ahead to see what your work schedule is like, so you can study for exams or complete homework assignments on time. Working boosted my confidence. It helped me stay on top of my studies because I knew that my on campus job was helping pay for my education and the bills.

A job, while handling classes amongst other extracurriculars, tends to look good on the resume. The additional source of cash inflow makes it easier on yourself to occasionally splurge and treat yourself once in a while. In college, it's important not to get overwhelmed by your studies, and enjoy yourself every once in a while. However, if a job gets in the way of the quality of your grades too much, you may want to lower the number of hours you work, or not work at all, and shift your priorities to schoolwork instead. Only work as much as you can handle. Too much stress coming solely from work can put a damper on your grades and lifestyle. Work-life, or work-life-study, balance is critical in maintaining healthy relationships with others and a healthy lifestyle for yourself.

SAVING

If you are able to save in college, imagine how much easier it will be to save when you actually start making money when you graduate. Saving money habits are as important as ever to form early on. Culture has shifted to spending more than what you make. Pop culture, or the common approach to handling matters, is not always the right way to approach situations. Far too many people are living life in a mountain of debt they can never climb out of. Saving spare money will prevent you from financial problems in the long-term.

An emergency fund is critical for, you guessed it, emergencies. This means you should not put your hand in the cookie jar if your emergency fund is reaching a limit you want it to reach. Starting an emergency fund in college makes it a great practice to get you out of sticky situations. You are not going to fail at budgeting if you don't have an emergency fund in place during college because loans and family members will hopefully be there to assist you. When it gets to adulthood, not having an emergency fund can you put you in more of a bind than you realize. You could have your house foreclosed on. If an emergency takes away from your regular fixed costs, food, car payments, insurance, medical expenses could all be a struggle to be pay for.

Right now, you are getting several things at a discounted rate because you are a college student. It definitely does not seem like it since tuition, room, and board expenses keep rising, but it is true. Once you leave college, you may no longer have a roommate to split those housing costs with. You don't realize the full extent of what paying bills are until you are completely separated from relying on your parents or guardians. The only envelopes I get in the mail anymore are different sorts of bills to pay. Saving up money can help cover those increased costs.

As I'm sure you have learned in finance classes by now, money can work for you without you having to do anything. A term called compound interest does the trick. Keeping money in a piggy bank for a rainy day is not a bad idea, but that money does not grow, it stays the same amount as you put it in the piggy bank. What if you put it in a Savings account instead? You could earn interest on top of the money you have put in the Savings account, and eventually, you will be earning interest on top of that interest you have earned. In order for this to take effect in noticeable amounts, you will have to wait a few years to notice any reasonable change.

I use a Savings account called Marcus by Goldman Sachs. It's simple. It's an online savings account that I can track, and it grows at 2.25% APY. (Annual Percentage Yield-An annual rate of return, accounting for compound interest.) It requires no monthly fees and no minimum amount to get started, plus it's FDIC insured since it's a bank. The money grows at 2.25% yearly without me having to do a single thing. While investing in stocks would give you a better chance to get a higher return, the Marcus Savings account return is guaranteed with little to no risk.

EMBRACING THE FREEDOM

If you feel crunched for money and your monthly bills are adding up on non-essential items, look to what the university is offering you for free just by being a student. Sign up for campus email lists (hopefully the lists that don't bog you down with thousands of emails) that give a calendar of events happening on campus. Many times, depending on how big the university is, they'll have a group of students and staff specifically in charge of hosting activities and fun nights for students. Join trivia nights with friends and attend free movie showings and concerts all at the university's expense. Since you're paying for it indirectly through tuition and student fees towards the college, you might as well take advantage of all the freebies it throws at you. Student gym memberships are a bonus as well. The student membership discount was always cheaper than any other non-university affiliated program. I would learn how to take care of my body and mind with advice from the university's wellness coordinators and learn how to push my body in all sorts of ways with fitness classes, from yoga to cardio kickboxing to Zumba. And let me tell you, if you're a boy looking to interact with the ladies, a Zumba class is a fantastic way to break the ice and get a sweat on at the same time.

GroupOn is fantastic for when you and your friends are bored and need something to do that won't break the budget. From concert and comedy showings, to bowling and escape room activities, there's a broad range of fun for anyone to find something to do and save some money doing it.

College kids tend to party from time to time, a shocker I know. You may go out with your friends from time to time; the casual hangout every few weeks to multiple times a week. Be sure that the money you are using is not the money you may need to use for essential things. Definitely set aside that work or allowance money to go out and have some fun.

If you have a problem swiping your credit card with no shame in spending, use cash only when you go out. When you see that cash leave your hand, you feel a bit more sensitive as to what you're purchasing. Credit cards can make it seem as though you have unlimited money at times.

Use that work money or that money saved up to live a little and experience things out of your normal routine. When they say your college years will fly by, they aren't kidding. Embrace the freedom and enjoy the opportunities ahead. You will never again have the chance to experience the opportunities you receive in college when you enter adulthood.

POST-GRAD REFLECTION

Be sure to look back on your experiences. We can get so caught up in the hustle of life that we lose track of the progress we've made. This serves well in the midst of tough times. Major projects, final exams, and long writing assignments can break you down. Reflect on how far you have come. You are building a foundation for your future by how you handle college and all the obstacles it throws your way.

Post-graduation is the time to evaluate your financial successes and downfalls the past few years as an undergraduate. This is the time to grow off of the financial maturity you have established. Maybe you want to purchase a house right out of college. Maybe you want to get a new car and not use the beater car that got you through college by the skin of your teeth. All you know is what you have practiced. The practical steps you take as you go through your schooling years can be applied to lifelong situations. When you are aware of your finances, you think more about your long-term success of being financially secure and independent.

By following a budget plan and really sticking to it, you can easily monitor your progress. Reflect on those plans where you guesstimated your budget correctly. Learn from the times your actual expenses went way beyond your guesstimated expenses. Oops. Positive reflection is a way to grow from those past experiences. Failures can actually reveal a lot more than successes. View failures as an experiment and your end goal as being successful. The end goal is to have a budget plan in place that serves as a foundation for your future financial success.

Reflecting back can be quite arduous at times. It may seem like a waste of time. It may initially seem like you have nothing to gain from the past. However, if you really look back at your budget and spending habits of the past, you develop wisdom for the future. Devote your time, focus, and attention to reflecting on yourself. Your plans will never be perfect. You can only learn how to get better. College flies by. Meeting new friends, learning new material, having many new opportunities arise is just the beginning. For the first time, you really don't have any restrictions besides the discipline you've grown up with. It's a time for you to take control of your own experiences. Take the driver's seat in your college lifestyle. Take control of your budget. It's simple to set a budget plan for yourself. College is not the time to put yourself on airplane mode. College is the time to do extraordinary things with your budget and with your life because you'll never get a chance quite like it again.

WORKS CITED

Freedman, Liz. "The Pennsylvania State University Division of Undergraduate Studies." *The Mentor*, 2013, dus.psu.edu/mentor/2013/06/disconnect-choosing-major/.

Carter, Matt. "What Is the Average Student Loan Debt After College?" *Credible*, 25 Mar. 2019, www.credible.com/blog/statistics/average-student-loan-debt-statistics.

Best Schools. "21 Scary Facts About College." *TheBestSchools.org*, Thebestschools.org, 18 Oct. 2016, thebestschools.org/magazine/21-scary-facts-college/.

"What Are the Different Types of Financial for College Students?" *CollegeQuest*, 16 July 2014, www.collegequest.com/different-types-of-financial-aid-for-college.aspx.